// Please read carefully.

Possible side effects include: a previously latent aversion to intimacy, and distrust of life jackets; buses at the periphery of your vision, and compulsive waving; papyrophobia, and blindness to the suffering of others; extreme fluctuations in weight, and extreme fluctuations in age; a compulsion to assume victimhood, and a tendency to blame the victim; mass deforestation, and coastal erosion. If you experience any side effects, including those not listed, talk to your doctor, nurse, pharmacist, priest, or reflection. The manufacturers cannot, and will not, be held responsible.

Use only as directed. //

First published 2019 by The Hedgehog Poetry Press

Published in the UK by
The Hedgehog Poetry Press
Coppack House, 5
Churchill Avenue
Clevedon
BS21 6QW

www.hedgehogpress.co.uk

ISBN: 978-1-916480-60-5

Cover image © Oz Hardwick

Author Photograph © Susan Whitehouse

The Lithium Codex

//

Oz Hardwick

Contents

AUTUMN SCHEDULE

The window only opens a crack, but it's enough to let
the world in, with all its practiced diagnoses and passive-
aggressive concern. It sits too close, asks if I've been
looking after myself, comments on my weight loss, feigns
interest. Running its fingers through the dust on the TV,
it suggests housework, cooking, decluttering;
recommends exercise, yoga, a beach holiday, a new
career, cosmetic surgery, a fairy godmother. I'm used to
its tottering concerns – precarious as Jenga on a pitching
ship, swaying, ready to tip at the slip of a nervous breath
– so I close the window: but the world's still here, its
head pressed cold to my lap like a dead seal, suggesting
the 24-hour shopping channel; recommending a higher
dose.

LITHIUM SOUNDTRACK I

Everything is song, from the birds to the bricks: houses sing favourites from the early 80s, lyrics gaining strata of meaning in retrospect. He phones his dead mother to hear her answerphone voice, and she sings back lines from Hoagy Carmichael, Spike Jones. Under any other circumstance, he would join in and dance, but the whistling postman won't stop feeding junkmail through the letterbox – takeaways, estate agents, book clubs, broadband, cosmetic dentistry, adoption services, antidepressants, window cleaners – their contesting chatter crushing him into the sofa. If this was a musical, their voices would coalesce into the uplifting finale; if it was an action movie, he'd burn the muthas down; if it was Sci-Fi, he'd wake up in a million years. The songs get louder and the clock misses a beat.

THE NATURE OF THE CATASTROPHE

The first real frost of the year, and roofs are patterned like cows, steaming in the morning sun. The car coughs, refuses to start, so I begin the long walk through lanes that have changed overnight into Edwardian photographs of themselves, sharp but featureless, devoid of people. By the time I reach the office, it's summer, and I see myself, aged five or six, queueing for an ice-cream on an endless beach of castles and flags. Mum waves from a deckchair, but Dad is busy digging a moat, while my sister, her legs a sunburnt blur, runs towards the distant sea. My hands are wrinkled, but still cold, and shake as I buy a coffee. The lift jams between floors, and all I can hear are seagulls, rising waves.

STRAY

Beside the path, grass is temptation, moist in its green allure. We are here by mistake, our tongues having slipped while pronouncing our botanical devotions: if flowers have a language, it is parapraxis and ambiguous gesture, coded degrees of silence, their Victorian locutions quaint but bitter. It is raining names, but each is swallowed by greedy loam before we can grasp its inflections, leaving only fractured outlines, like the painted signs of businesses – ironmongers, saddleries and the like – that ghost the complexions of luxury flats, or the last bloom of a bruise you caught in the dark, searching for water in a house that burst with somniloquy. Against these confusions, we do what we can, blinkering ourselves in blue kagoules, watching our steps in single file, keeping off the grass.

BRANCH LINE

I sleep on stations out of choice, preferring their absences and nuances to the certainty of home. In the waiting room, the gas fire hisses to itself, reflecting back its history from dirty windows. I stretch across hard plastic seats, bunching my coat under my head so I can watch the spiders constructing their gothic halls in the corner, ribbed arches soaring from wall to ceiling. In my pocket, I carry a toothbrush and a lock of my mother's hair, kept safe against all eventualities, and folded pages from favourite novels that I read in different orders to surprise myself and find my bearings. Outside may not exist, but if it does, there are skeletons of steam trains nosing the platforms for coal, a lamp-lighter as thin as his tidy flame, and a marble-white woman, naked at the news stand, waiting for the signals to change.

HAPPY

Commemorations accrete like gases, responding to gravity, creating atmospheres: they cool over time and change states. On this day, The Beatles switched from leather jackets to smart suits, mid-set, deep in Liverpool's bombed-out heart, but the website I browse at breakfast has more deaths, from Cozy Powell to Kurt Cobain, and I wonder why so few ghosts are reported, and why none of them wears denim. It's the same with births, and my sense of divine order needs a Roger Corman biopic of Thomas Hobbes, with Spencer Tracy and a Dave Swarbrick soundtrack: but in a remote field where cities can't swallow stars, Donald Lynden-Bell presses his ghostly eye to a brass telescope to watch Renate Bruemmer's aerial ballet, falling in love with her effortless assemblés and arabesques, the glint from her tinted visor. There are countless other worlds, where different laws apply, but I pick up this small memorial stone between my thumb and forefinger, inspect it in today's new light, and commit it to memory.

FIT FOR WORK

Late at night, I get a text from a friend I haven't seen for maybe a year. He asks how I am, and I think of how we sat outside a station bar, drinking the local beer. He had an album in a specialist music chart and an E-cigarette that looked like plumbing equipment: I had a new book out and a pocket full of credit card receipts. We talked about the geographies that remember us as if we were lost children; that will claim us back sooner or later, offering hot soup and sturdy boots. In his text, he mentions someone I don't think I've met, who had his benefits cut off: maybe he was deemed fit for work. It makes me think how I'd just returned to work from a long illness, in which I'd been buried in the cellar of a house on the coast, tended by all the women from three generations of my family as my body's geology shifted, destabilising foundations; and how my friend had once heard the Devil in a far-off land, and how he still knew that voice, and how any empty chair could be tainted with brimstone. The text explains how, with the support cut off, there had been nothing left, and how my friend was at the funeral earlier. And it reminds me that I caught the train home, but that, as always, I never arrived.

SELF-ASSESSMENT

It is 11.30am. Amongst the creases, a succession of
questions, an unfolding scenario: How will I recognise
success? Mum answers the door, appearing drowsy,
dishevelled and still in pyjamas. Is it too late to be
wearing pyjamas, or is she immobile at the door, like that
statue in the fountain, where rainbows danced and split
like revelation, though all I could think of was: What is
a rainbow called when caused by something other than
rain? What methods will I use to achieve my learning
objectives? The house was cold and the room was untidy
with rubbish, dirty plates and cups around the room.
Details are picked out, but the unnecessary repetition of
room reminds me we are considering a domestic space
here, regardless of the current disarray: someone lives
here – *has to* live here – with all their questions sticking
in the carpet, pasted beneath the wallpaper, and blowing
in on scribbled notes each time the window is opened. I
flatten out another sheet: How will I practise and apply
what I learn?

ALL MY SHOES

All my shoes are different sizes but fit perfectly. I line them up in the parquet hall, first in pairs, but then in size order, biggest towards the door, smallest towards the stairs. There's a trainer between brogues, a walking shoe so far from its mate that initially I miss it, and so on. You get the idea. My first thought is that I didn't realise I had so many shoes and there are, to be honest, some that I should throw away: but this is missing the point. Let me be clear, I'm not doing micro-measurements here: we're talking about significant differences that I could spot from a distance even without my glasses. They form a long, slightly curving wedge, like a coastal bight, where each sole-squeak on the floor is a gull circling above a small boat leaving home for the last time, its huddled passengers scared, upset, but hopeful as they huddle close, watching the land recede. Blink, and it's a marimba, its deep tones bubbling through the whole house until it looses its moorings and floats into a sky the colour of police lights, scattering those flap-happy gulls. By way of experiment, I close my eyes and pick two shoes at random from opposite ends of the line, not even checking for left and right. They are an exact match and fit perfectly.

WHEELS

Bike wheels whip through rainbows, urban fountains in Victorian piazzas. We are free today – but maybe not tomorrow – maybe never again – and alive to the city's stretch and curve, its subtleties of stone and glass. We move like birds, buoyed on currents of commerce and industry, buffeting afternoon shoppers, spinning through lanes. On days like this we own everything we see, everything we remember, though our feelings are only borrowed from the novels we read aloud in your narrow attic bed. It's enough, as we pedal beside the canal, across burgeoning fields, past farms, mills and mines, sticky with watermelon sugar, golden in the dripping sun.

NEWS JUST IN

There's a drumming in the library, a rattle in the courthouse, a roll in the gait of the drunk schoolteacher trying to forget equations. The tabloids trumpet babies and bananas, unremarkable weather for the time of year, the disintegration of diplomacy and celebrity marriages. Invisible strings tie kids to particular streets, beating the medieval bounds, policing the margins of future apologies. And the radio shakes to the beat of mines and speeding tickets, flat Yorkshire vowels, speculation regarding manned missions to Mars.

CARTOGRAPHY

Even in an hourglass, sand is a kind of map, its shifting
significations showing where to go and what to avoid, so
I have become a cartographer, nibbing new contours
with each reconfiguration. Getting things wrong takes a
steady hand, precise flexions and a calm pulse: post
offices become libraries, museums become motels,
swimming pools become cinemas, and everything else is
just fire hydrants and speed cameras. It's the same when
we cross borders or cross each other behind our backs:
symbols could mean anything, and landscapes fold in on
themselves, while nobody takes time to read the Legend,
assuming we know better.

RECALIBRATING THE MAREOGRAPH

When we swim, we breathe sand: when we build, we layer water upon water. We carry the coast wherever we go, widening intractable marches, building contested borders into the grammar of habitual actions. I collect shells that wash up on mountainsides, set them in their most musical order, parse their evolving relationships, and sew them into the hems of billowing silk pavilions. You long for the dead certainty and tidy edges of a Comfort Zone I don't recognise and can't even imagine without feeling its bricks crushing my eyelids, its mortar hardening in my veins. I try to convince you that sand and water are nothing but linguistic categories: you tell me we're out of our element, as if that's a bad thing, as if we should choose cells over diving boards or straight-jackets over wings – as if we knew the way home, and believed it was still there.

LAST ORDERS

There are fires on the hillside, promises in the drawer, and I will myself to care about either. It's after chucking-out time, and remnants of conversations thread into sloping streets, punctuated by cats and closing doors, ending in dream-dashed sleep and muscle cramps; but someone has to watch for change, so I gulp sweet coffee and check star charts for anomalies. What used to be figurative has become a kind of fact – a commonplace, even – and just as there is nothing of love in fire, so locked letters are nothing but ink on paper, the occasional photograph; yet still there is no warmth, no fuel, and the drunken street talk becomes louder the further it recedes, and the only things that make sense are cramps and closing doors.

AFTER HOURS

In the cellar bar, deep sea divers sip neat spirits, speak
in bubbles. A mermaid pulls pints that darken dimpled
glasses. Look: this is truth, not physics, so barnacles
crowd the pinball machines as an octopus cheats at pool,
surreptitiously pocketing spots as he lines up the pink.
I've been here so long that my fingers have swelled into
sea cucumbers, prime for the perfect crime, stealing
time and leaving unreadable prints on the clock casing.
It's my round as it strikes 1am, and I am watching the
stairs as the mermaid tips the bottle, spoons tiny
icebergs, anticipates the next wreck and its dazed
survivors.

A BRIEF HISTORY OF MERMAIDS

History, you tell me, is written by the swimmers; by the fin-fisted negotiators of time and truth – axes which float like Pooh-sticks beached beneath a crumbling bridge. Last night I dived into our divided past, into your underwater Titanic wedding – not the Grand Ballroom, with its plucky orchestra still playing, but the limpet-strewn steerage half-light, with all its desperate bustle and rehearsed apology. You had framed your own mirror, sewn your own scales, combed your hair until it wrapped around the deep reflected moon. One of your silverslim pages was your own son, though in the bluegreen ripple I wasn't sure which one. It was nothing like the day we lay tangled, becalmed beneath dead branches in a drifting skiff, wet limbs twisting and brittle as coral; but I woke up knowing it was still a matter of tides and their negotiations, the balance between trust and breathing, and the incessant pull of the deep.

PAPER ROSES

Maybe this isn't the time for meaningful glances and scented billets-doux, but the mist off the river has other ideas, nudging back the clock until I find myself in an Edwardian coming-of-age novel, with all its overgrown melancholy and prim desires. There's a steam train with a soldier waving, a hothouse gripped tight by vines, charcoal nannies perambulating silent babies, and every chimney holds the bones of a nameless waif who now sings in the whitest heaven that ever sailed the Empire. I am learning starched manners and the art of not speaking, becoming over-sensitive to the flow of bright fabric and the fall of a loose curl, bedazzled by the possible implications of a casual word or the precise angles of wrist and cheek. The library shimmers with gas lamps, rings with polite china, and sighs with linen against skin. The mist presses its face against the window, and I am sick with roses as I press myself between the pages of the family Bible.

CRIME SCENE

When you describe the smell of discovered bodies, I think about the way that carpets always grow the same patterns in the end, the way that the viewpoint of the photographic image is moving towards the aesthetic of the crime scene. For all the TV documentaries, I still compare myself, generally unfavourably, with chalked outlines on pavements. You never blanch, never have to swallow bile, and you tell me you never have, yet you grip my arm like a trap in the cinema with each telegraphed shock. There you are again, hung from the smoke between burning buildings, unconscious of the mechanics ticking beneath your uniform. You meet death every night, and tonight will be no different. As you note the exit wound or the dangling needle, you will weigh up contents of bookcases, integrity of décor, sell-by dates in fridges; and later, I will consider your outline, white against whatever else you carry home.

Walking on water's easy once you have the knack; just a matter of knowing when to shift the weight from one foot to the other before it breaks the surface. I learnt it in those dog days when the ship (if you could call it a ship – at what point does a ship become a boat?) stuck like a spider in paint, motionless beneath an unwavering sun. It was a woman who worked in the kitchen (do they call it a galley? or is that Romantic antiquarianism these days?) who taught me. We'd wait until late, when the ship/boat was sleeping, and I'd follow her widdershins (*purely for effect,* she told me, winking), splashing and gulping while she patiently padded on dainty feet that barely got wet, until I finally caught her on faltering steps, and we wrapped ourselves in each other's arms, stifling laughter so as not to wake the sleepers. You see, it's easy once you have the knack: it just takes time and patience. Come on – follow me.

More than language, I covet sand, each grain a world under the microscope, each plane curled out like a cat's paw stretching in my lap. It's a trap easily avoided, but one that never fails: the bird's head severed in the undergrowth, the broken sunglasses. Scrolling through photos later, all I can see are reflections, all objects having lost themselves in themselves, all angles having been covered. More than sand, I covet the tide which – Cnut in reverse – I will to remain; yet it still recedes, steady, revealing shells, rocks, debris, wrecks, and a lost kingdom ruled by a bird-headed god who speaks perfect English, enigmatic in sunglasses which were dropped from a tourist boat in 1974.

HORSES

Take it straight from the horse's mouth: the grass isn't greener – it isn't grass at all. It's the tyres on wet gravel, the shadows of daffodils in dipped headlights. It's the uneven steps of erosion and drunkenness, each curving higher into darkness. It's the words that slip between a cupped palm and the lip of the abyss. It's the uncertainty of ages in near-forgotten guidebooks that may have been for somewhere else entirely. It's the assumption of myth, and its nettle sting that no leaves can ease. But it is not grass, and it has never been grass: take it straight from the horse's mouth – but if it's a gift, don't look.

EVENING IN GLASS

Evening falls over, an early drunk, mumbling mild profanities over the high street. We've been here before: a bar with uncomfortable chairs, cryptic flyers on low tables, and beers with dumb names. If I could draw my life back into the taps, I'd say something stupid about the curl of hair around your ear, the slapstick sequence of mistakes that have led me to avoid your eyes as I describe the evolving arc of a heron's flight over the valley in the last light. But evening picks itself up, dusts itself down, threatens at the window. And I sip my beer carefully, so as not to loosen those perfect words from where they hide in plain sight of anyone but you.

At the edges, our skin grows feathers, tentative wings assessing the weight of air, the consistency of everything that is not us. It grows curious, loving its own curve and dance, the discomfort that assures it of both its mortality and immortality, and of the space that is no space between the two. As soon as we touch we are changed, an Ovidian twist into flight and a chorus of sealight, an unshuttering of arbitrary distinctions between senses. Because at the edges there are no edges: have you ever felt such luminous song?

THE WEIGHT OF LIGHT

The weight of light geared the intricate machine. A shifting matrix of cogs, wires and shining spheres, it turned, silent as smoke, through unresisting time, as we stood spellbound, anticipating beginnings and endings, a reshuffling of elements. If we could see our reflections, we didn't say, but I think we all looked beyond surfaces anyway, checking for deeper signs. *At what point,* I wondered, *does a simulacrum become real?* I reached out, felt a pulse, closed my fingers around its warm fluttering, and felt myself arc away like a hawk clutching its twilight prey.

OUT OF TURN

We act out of turn but no longer notice the signs, though we've played so long that the cards have worn to transparency. Nothing is hidden. It has become a habit we can't break, the shuffle and slide a sibilant soundtrack to everything we never say, while the stakes that were once so high have lost all value. Nothing is lost or won, but each time we face each other across the worn table, I fold.

FLAME GRAMMAR

Swift as ash we sift through litter for the bitter words we wish we hadn't lost, their sounds crumpling at the bases of lampposts like a rejected drawing from a children's chapbook. When your texts arrive, they burn my fingers, melting their whorls into the plastic screen – the kind of outcome that insurance policies don't account for – and I long for the simpler days of smouldering postcards, of demands nailed to my bedroom door. We'd probably speak, but our mouths are full of cinders, and anything we say could be taken down and used to torch remote villages, so we flick the grey dust to and fro, to and fro, listening with our guts for casual greetings and imprecations, the parapraxis of flame grammar that flares like a shameful rash.

THE LAST LETTER

The last letter is written on maple leaves, maybe gathered from a northern fall, maybe cut from a book. It's written in a child's neat hand, in haste, in a cartridge pen bought at the corner shop, where a bursting poke of sweets cost threepence, and where identical twins sorted magazines and model kits. There were more identical twins in those days, and most of them ran shops, like the cobblers and key-cutters, the electricians who sold hand-blown Christmas lights in the shapes of parrots and devils. Time is not an animal, but still it howls in the night, presses its hungry snout at the horologist's window, tears at leaves and letters, with just this one remaining: it is addressed to someone else.

LITHIUM SOUNDTRACK II

A mattress on the floor and towers of unshelved books. The night slips through another crack in the floorboards, a Sinatra melody that lives in your head though you've not heard it since you can't remember when. Empty bottles and dregs in glasses. The room's full of shapes that anyone else would find threatening, but your skin feels like your own for the first time, and the dawn can't step over the threshold until you invite it in.

NOTICE TO QUIT

Symptom or side effect? There are days when I long to be the spent matchsticks still lying in the hearth from last winter, so I throw away everything from the kitchen cupboards and press my palm to the candle flame until it freezes, carve away my imagined flesh with nothing but water, judge my bones wanting when they shuffle into the wardrobe mirror. Madness or medication? There are words I laugh at when I spit them out - *crazy, nutter, psycho* - the same words I have tattooed on my back in invisible ink like a *kick me* notice on April Fools' Day: *sticks and stones*, and all that, but these words beat and burn. Kill or cure? The grate is empty of all but dust and voices, my body is empty of all but scars and words, and discarded blister packs are empty of all but inevitable futures.

THE NINTH WAVE

Waves break the line between sleep and awake, and I am bruised and confused, lying on the floor. I remember turning to my mother, then turning to my father, our mouths open in almost speech – fish astonished by a rupture in surface tension – with tidal questions concerning the precise nature and location of city and coast, of our shared memories of division. All things are relative, though relatives are only rarely all things; but we're all artists of one kind or another, and whoever was first to blink turned Lowry to Hokusai, penning sharp edges. Before the wave fell, I squeezed my eyes shut, felt the hammer of compressed air and the absence of divisions. It may take weeks for the bruises to fade, and I doubt I'll ever know where exactly the fault lines fall.

THE INSOMNIA CIRCUIT

For ten days and nights, I waited for stone, for flesh, for the whisper of blood. Condensation became sweat, became moss, became a small world, with all its triumphs and tragedies, soft beneath my fingers. Sundial circuits massaged our faces, a steady motion drawing wakefulness and sleep in their due seasons, a temperate enfolding of each hour. A deeper marriage, we shared marble dreams, the sympathy of veins, something like a pulse or a fever. For ten days without natural sleep, I lay with my cheek to her marble breast, listening to a heartbeat that could have been anyone's.

AMATEUR DRAMATICS IN THE PROVINCES

Her heart is a toy theatre, a cat's cradle, a skipping game played alone. Scenery slides in receding cardboard vistas of bushes, birds and distant towers, each hand-coloured, tight within the lines, as she locks her fingers in small rituals of patience and string. Protagonists are stiff as archetypes, adopting the gestures of garden statuary, but still awkward in their assigned roles. As her wrists flex, lattice shadows dissect customary plots she has cut from the family Bible and other myths, tricking discrete planes into hybridisation and metamorphosis, optical illusions of time and scale. If there were words, she would speak them now, but the elastic on her ankle is twisted, pulling her back, threatening to topple her into her childhood stage; and she knows that, the minute the painted branch breaks, the cradle will fall.

COMPASS

She hums the tunes of birds on wires, foxes on railway lines, guano on solar panels. Like everything else, synaesthesia is a spectrum, and I hear her songs like tumbling pastel shapes on a reception class floor. On my first day at school I built wooden roads that wove through sand and water but always headed North. There was a compass in my shoe, the Green Knight's blazon deep in my pocket, an explorer's eye on the horizon. Walking the paths of dead heroes, I didn't feel the cold, but that one song cut through my hand-knitted jumper, my unblemished skin. Circles, squares, triangles tip and roll, carved from sound, and the road still stretches on. She sings and I follow: I may be gone some time.

ODYSSEY

My face doubles in the train window: four eyes, two
mouths, twice as many years. On the mudflats is the
corpse of a boat, picked to bones by gulls and salt, like a
wrecked nest or a robot hand from a pulp Edwardian
novel in which the plucky heroine foils the attack with a
cunningly applied hat pin and a smile, the etching
emphasising the wry dimple in her high-boned cheek.
I've left these books behind for the house clearers to
parcel up and sell by length or weight, their spines
reduced to wallpaper, behind which that same heroine
will gather her modest grey skirt to run after the train I
left on hours ago, heading north, my face nodding into
its repeated self, multiplying distance from my
abandoned nest and a ghost ship sailing nowhere.

MISTAKEN IDENTITY

Winter caught up with me between the theatre and the railway station, slipped its arm in mine like we were old friends, and picked up a conversation that belonged to neither of us. We spoke about the birds on the red list, books on the black list, the comfort neither of us had ever found in strangers. We stopped to listen to a busker – or a policeman, or the river singing beyond the locked park gates – but when I dipped into my pocket for change, all I found were hailstones and clipped tickets for cloakrooms and provincial zoos.

PROBABILITY

Probably the world won't end, but probably the war won't end either. It's just physics or the postal service, with everything changing addresses or chasing new locations through equal and opposite forces and the laws of acceleration and conservation. If the world = W and war = w, we can posit the values of memory (m) and cats (c), based on the standard deviation when we plot the number of retained love letters against their scent ($x \pm$ forgetting (f)). If we take into account the variables introduced by news (N), fake news (Fn), and statistics (S), we can therefore deduce that W is to some degree contingent on w (and vice-versa), and that the extent to which m and c are variable can be represented as a cat curled amongst dried hydrangea flowers and a TV unplugged at the wall. Probably.

LITHIUM SOUNDTRACK REPRISE

She forgets arrivals, but remembers every time she's left: the softly closing door, the cab to another station. She blinks through the window, transforming the morning into an old movie stuttering into life. There are still milk floats in this part of town, like rattling icebergs calving into sleeping streets, and paper boys cut between hedges, careful to let sleeping dogs lie. And she remembers a Christmas, snug in flannelette pyjamas, sipping hot milk, carefully peeling tape so as not to tear cartoon paper; the fire crackling, and everyone smiling – but she can't remember what was inside. It's 5am, and the rail tracks are staves on which early birds improvise songs. She looks to the point where they curve into nothing, begins to whistle, then stops.

AFTERWORD.

The Lithium Codex is a record of conversations: with the poets who join me for breakfast; with the dead who won't let me sleep; with all the loves who dare not speak their names; with the chemicals and compounds that were born inside, and those that are just passing through.